With his "Welcome Home" cake, at Grace-land following his release from the Army — March of 1960.

E L V I S

A GOLDEN TRIBUTE

by Emory Glade

robus books

P.O. Box 13819 • Wauwatosa, WI 53213

ISBN 0-88188-347-6

Elvis, age 11 (third row, far right), with Tupelo classmates.

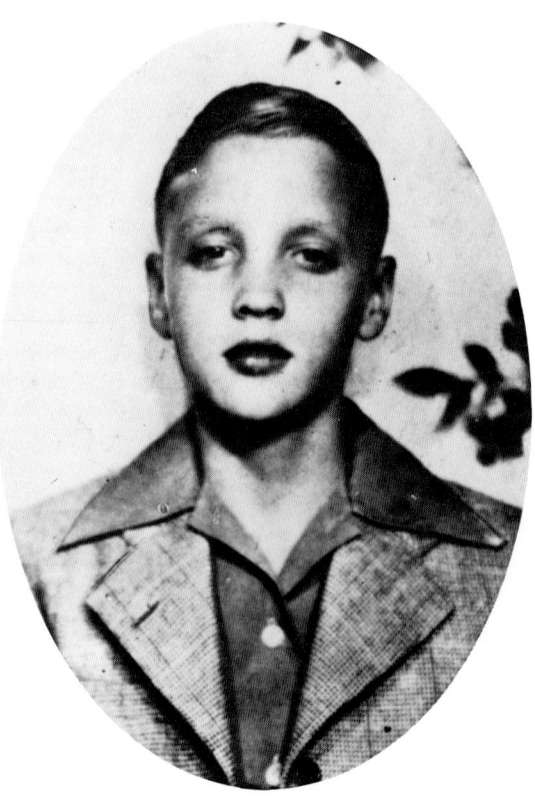

The dreamy-eyed twelve-year-old poses for a local photographer in Tupelo.

With a friend in Tupelo, before the family moved to Memphis in 1948.

Happy birthday, Elvis

It's hard to believe, but Elvis Aron Presley would have been fifty years old — half a century — on January 8, 1985, fifty years since the baby was born in the shotgun shack in Tupelo who would grow up to change forever the course of popular music throughout the world. Indeed, in every age, there are only a few individuals who manage, through extraordinary talent, power, ambition, and the machinations of history and destiny, to irrevocably change the lives of the nation and the society around them, to define an entire generation of Americans and then come to influence every subsequent generation. Such a man was Elvis Presley. Fifty years after his birth, seven years after his death, his influence only grows stronger, providing us with an opportunity to stop for a moment to appreciate just what this man has come to mean, and to celebrate his living legacy.

First, we have Elvis' music — a veritable treasure trove that ranges from his first, groundbreaking recordings with Sam Phillips at Sun Records in 1954 to his final release on RCA in 1977. But how to even begin to assess the impact of this body of work? Aside from countless gold, silver, and platinum records denoting hundreds of millions of records sold throughout the world, perhaps the best perspective we can use is the simple, undisputed moniker — royal title, even — that Elvis earned so early, by which he will always be known: *King of Rock and Roll.* Yes, King. There were other Great Ones during rock's Golden Age — Jerry Lee, Little Richard, Fats Domino, Chuck Berry, Buddy Holly — but because he alone created a veritable revolution in style, in consciousness, in the music business, and in the mainstream of American popular culture, Elvis Presley

GROWING UP

Rare photo of Elvis at seventeen, in 1952, sitting on the back steps of his parents' house at the Lauderdale Courts Apartments.

LIBRARY WORKERS

Back Row, left to right: Richard Flaniken, Billy Barber, George Makrus, Joe Coyle, Geraldine Barber, Herbert Blooming, Larry Holmes, Ralph Shinbaum, Charles Catros, Val Crotts, Elvis Presley.

Middle Row, left to right: Charlotte Young, Doris Varnavas, Ruth Mandelman, Joyce Beard, Billie May Chiles,

Louise Carson, Lillian Davis, Joan Liberts, Rachel Maddox, Joe Collins, Flois Gwaltney.

Front Row, left to right: Maureen Kapell, Nina Faverty, Jane Garey, Peggy Simmons, Norma Banks, Annie Varnavas, Billie Banks, Evelyn Hicks.

'ith fellow library workers, L.C. Humes High (back row, far right).

was raised up as the perfect living symbol of the new music sweeping the nation. Yes, to this drawling, sneering, gunk-haired Southern boy with the heavy-lidded blue eyes belonged the mantle of glory — fame, influence, riches beyond his wildest dreams — as well as what would become the burden of his office: the controversy, the denunciations, the constant scrutiny, the increasing isolation. . . . What he gave us was nothing less than immortal: the records he cut in 1954-1955 with Sam Phillips at Sun — "That's All Right (Mama)," "Milk Cow Blues Boogie," "Good Rocking Tonight," and "Mystery Train" among them — ushered in a new era of popular music with their combination of the style of country music with that of the blues, a style that would come to be known as "rockabilly." Then, when he signed with RCA, Elvis unleashed an unending stream of hit singles that exploded on the American scene like

concussion bombs — "Heartbreak Hotel," "Hound Dog," "Blue Suede Shoes," "Teddy Bear," "Don't Be Cruel," "Jailhouse Rock," "Love Me Tender" (the list goes on!) — which continued unabated until Elvis was inducted into the army in 1958 (and then actually kept going thanks to the shrewdness of Elvis' manager, Col. Tom Parker, who always kept enough music in the can to release records while Elvis wasn't recording).

These songs reveal Elvis as a remarkable vocalist — as a song stylist who didn't simply perform a song, but who had the uncanny ability to interpret his music and then personalize it to a point of unprecedented power and feeling. Again, this is because Elvis was no mere singer, no mere entertainer. Here we leave the easily understandable turf of music and enter the realms of his background, character, images, dreams, and of the

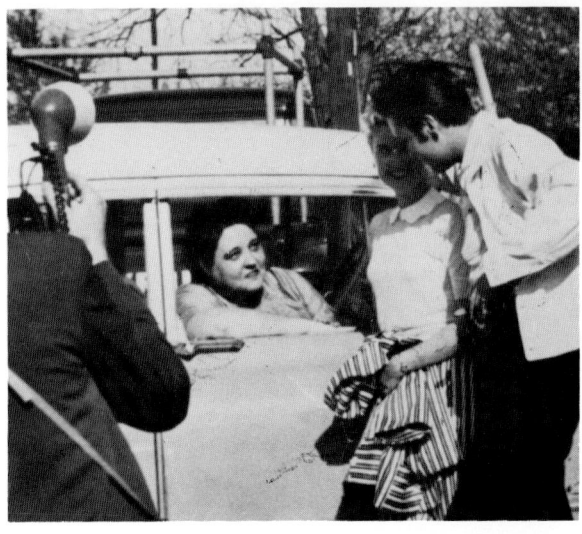

Elvis, Gladys, and Vernon — happy days before his mother's chronic health problems became worse.

country and people he came to personify. For if ever a musical figure came to symbolize his country, it was Elvis.

How did this happen and why? He was a country boy, dirt poor, who came to Memphis, went to high school like everybody else, and dreamed of making it big in order to have the kind of life that every American dreams about. Music was his vehicle for everything he wanted, everything he wanted to become, and if there is one discernible characteristic of his music that sets it apart and gives it real power, it must be the naked emotion he was able to put into his music, whether a lilting ballad or a raucous, lusty rocker. Elvis didn't just sing a song; he *felt* a song, and thus his audience was able to feel his music.

And when he began moving to the music, gyrating, swivelling, popping, and shaking, that was how he felt; like

breaking free. The rest of Young America during the fifties, of course, quickly adopted him as theirs — as their own vehicle for rebellion and liberation from the bland stodginess of that conformist decade, and from the current sexual, social, and racial constraints. For this reason, Elvis was "dangerous" to the older generation, to the establishment who saw him as a whirling dervish of sex, as the ruination of everything they held sacred. He could be so good and so bad at the same time; a truly American paradox, a walking mass of contradictions. Ah, but it keeps getting deeper. . . .

His music became the soundtrack for an entire era, and his appeal quickly extended beyond the shores of this country. The earthquake he created was felt everywhere and changed lives: Scores of other rockers found their paths made easier by his

GLADYS & VERNON

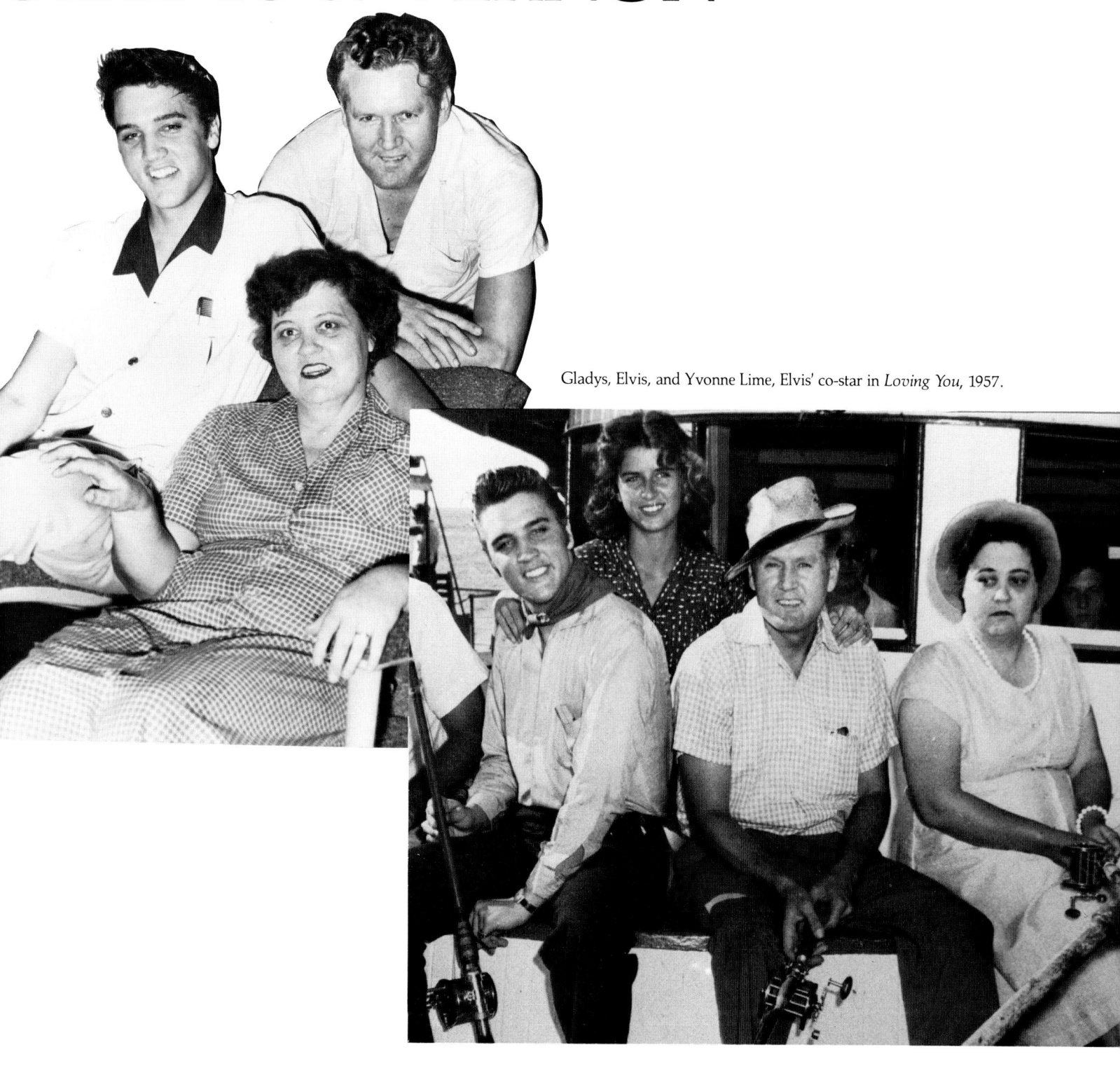

Gladys, Elvis, and Yvonne Lime, Elvis' co-star in *Loving You*, 1957.

example and success: a new generation grew up listening to him. (In Liverpool, for instance, a teenager named John Lennon would remember the first time he heard Elvis as the most crucial moment of his life.) And when rock's third generation began coming of age in the seventies and eighties, the influence of Elvis was no less profound. Artists wanted to sing like him, look like him, dance like him. Some, like new wave crooner Elvis Costello, even wanted his name!

Still, the legacy of Elvis Presley transcends the label of King of Rock and Roll. When Elvis went into the army and proved himself a model recruit, he broadened his audience still further. Hey, the guy may be a sexy rebel, but he also loves his mother, his country, God, apple pie, children, teddy bears, football, law and order — a philanthropist who gives lavishly to charities, a responsible citizen who cares about his public image and the values of his fans.

In this manner, Elvis was eventually able to conquer the very people who'd vilified him during his wild, early days. He became a folk hero, one of the first truly modern superstars of show business. An American institution. In Hollywood, he was a box-office sex symbol. The promise he showed as an actor in his first films *(Love Me Tender, Loving You, King Creole, Jailhouse Rock)* was thrown away following his release from the army when his manager settled on a money-making formula of low-budget vehicles that bored Elvis out of his wits but earned him millions, thanks to the remarkable loyalty of his fans. (What other film star could have made flics like *Harum Scarum* and walked away with a cool million and a half?)

Elvis and friend, letting it all hang out at 1034 Audubon Drive, 1956.

And then, just when it seemed that Elvis' career and influence were waning, along came his electrifying return to live performance, with his opening at the International Hotel in Las Vegas in August of 1969. Elvis emerged larger than ever and took his show on the road. The mature Elvis was even more eagerly consumed by his public. Indeed, the country boy, teen idol, and King of Rock and Roll may have seemed easy to grasp, but the mature superstar certainly wasn't. This superstar provided a little something for everybody. Elvis Presley somehow managed to combine an irresistible and purely American amalgamation of images and influences into a grand concoction of his own making.

Like America, Elvis was also a melting pot; his influences were like ingredients going into an astonishing blender, and the

mixture that resulted was his life. He managed to reflect the uniqueness and diversity of the vast country that loved him and made him what he was. Truckdrivers, farmers, singers, athletes, soldiers, movie stars, rebels, lovers, dreamers, sinners, and saints all found their way into his soul to become a part of him, and yet he could be all of them at once or none of them at all. Elvis was, well, *Elvis*. Just think of him in a white calfskin jumpsuit studded with precious stones, down on his knee, the sweat on his face glistening in the spotlight, singing "*Glory glory, Hallelujah. His truth goes marching on . . . .*"

Truly, this was no mere entertainer, but a myth, a legend, a symbol of what might have happened to any of us. Millions of his fans looked at him and thought, There, but for the grace of God, go I. He acted out, on the public stage, the hopes and fears

ELVIS

With one of his choppers, 1034 Audubon Drive, Memphis, 1956.

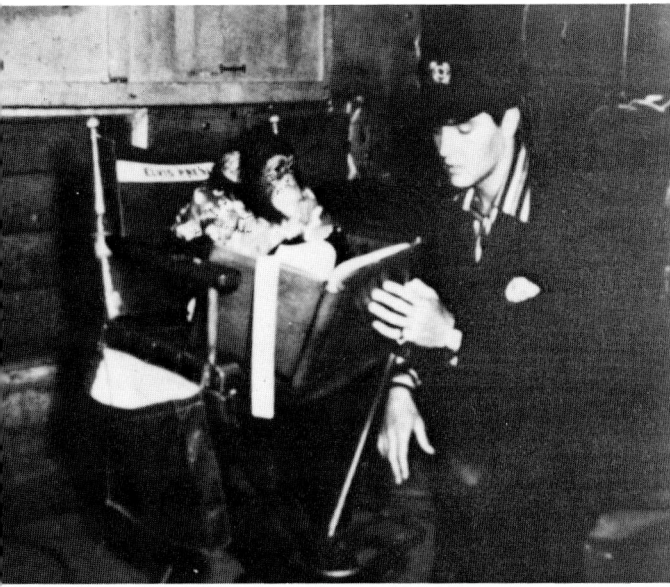

Elvis with his pet monkey, "Scatter," who provided Elvis and his entourage with endless opportunities for practical joking. (Elvis used to have the chimp chauffeured around in the back of a Rolls or limousine.)

and dreams of people who lived vicariously through him, who saw him as the purest incarnation of the American Dream.

Perhaps more than anything else, this realization helps to explain the worldwide response to Elvis' death on August 16, 1977 and the enduring public fascination with his life. Elvis had touched so many lives in so many different ways that his death seemed to evoke the deaths of John Kennedy and Rudolph Valentino and Judy Garland all at once, giving his life the monumental proportions of a great Shakespearean tragedy. By providing the kind of indelible memories by which we have come to measure our own lives, Elvis has given and continues to give a pure, simple joy to millions of people. On his fiftieth birthday, we celebrate him here in a collection of photos — Elvis as he really was, Elvis as we will always remember him.

IN THE ARMY

Private Presley, 1958.

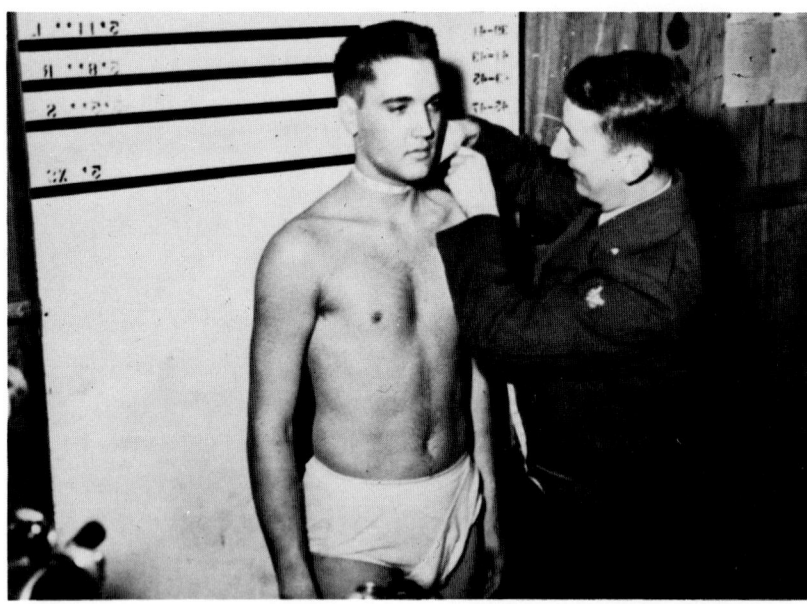

Induction into the army, March, 1958.

Warming up during maneuvers, Germany, 1959.

March, 1960. Elvis, recently released from the army, arrived at the Memphis station with Col. Parker.

Displaying his new sergeant's stripes, Germany, 1959.

Just days out of the army, Elvis en route to Miami for a Timex Special
at the Fountainbleu Hotel with Frank Sinatra, March 26, 1960.

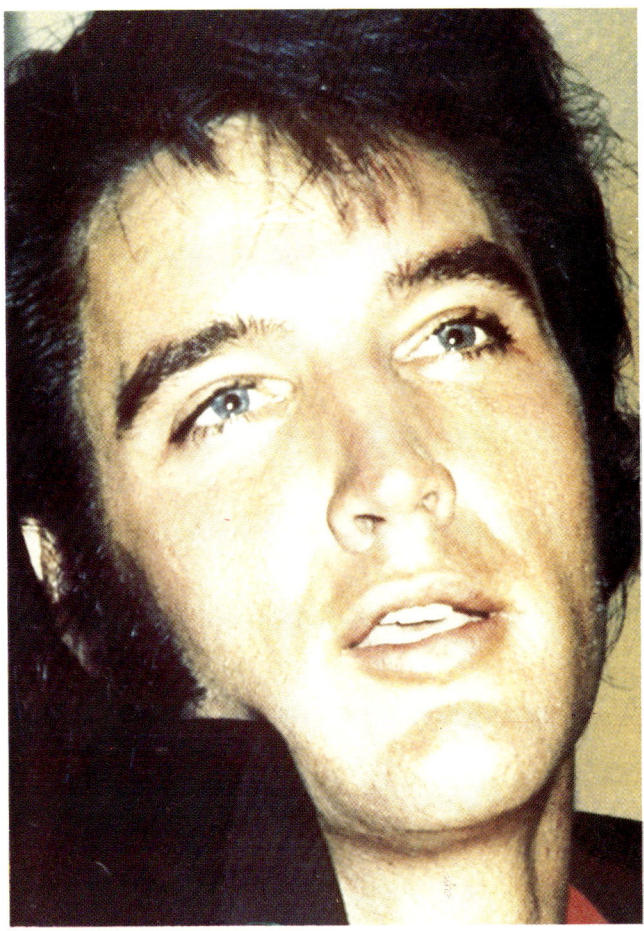

At press conference before his Las Vegas opening at the
International Hotel, July 31, 1969.

Elvis, 1956.

The famous "curled lip."

Elvis, dressed in traditional karate gi, applauds a karate instructor
in the Los Angeles studio of Ed Parker.

Dig those shoes! This photo was taken in 1957, while filming *Loving You*. Twenty-seven years later, these shoes are the rage . . .

Elvis on the set of *Jailhouse Rock*, Hollywood, 1957.

...N THE MOVIES

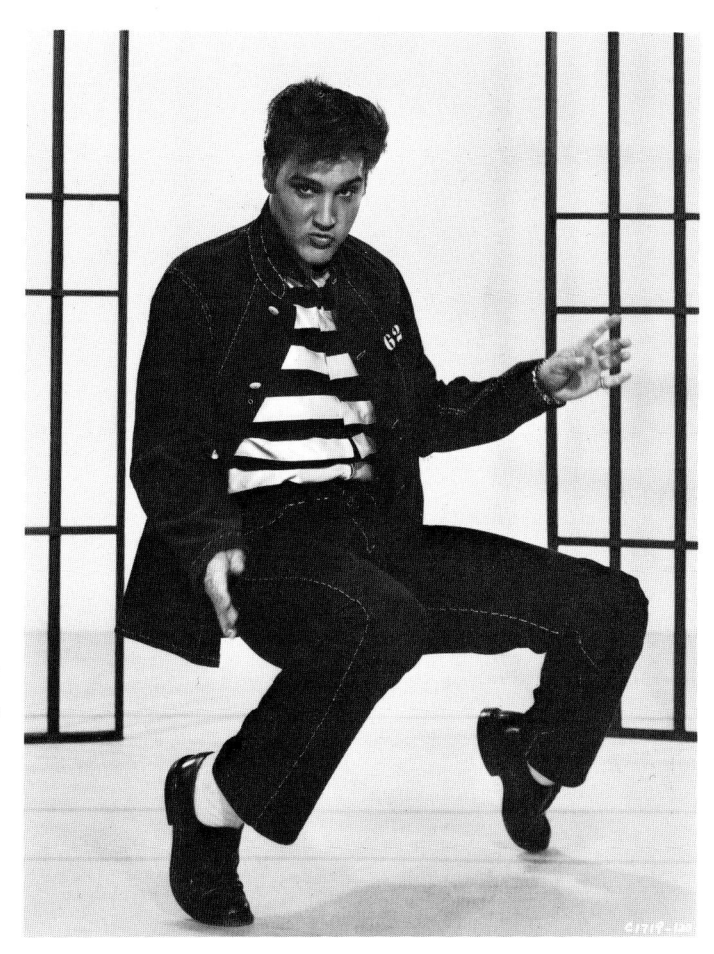

Jailhouse Rock

The famous dance sequence to the song "Jailhouse Rock," choreographed by Elvis himself for the 1957 film.

Smooching with Jennifer Holden in *Jailhouse Rock*, 1957.

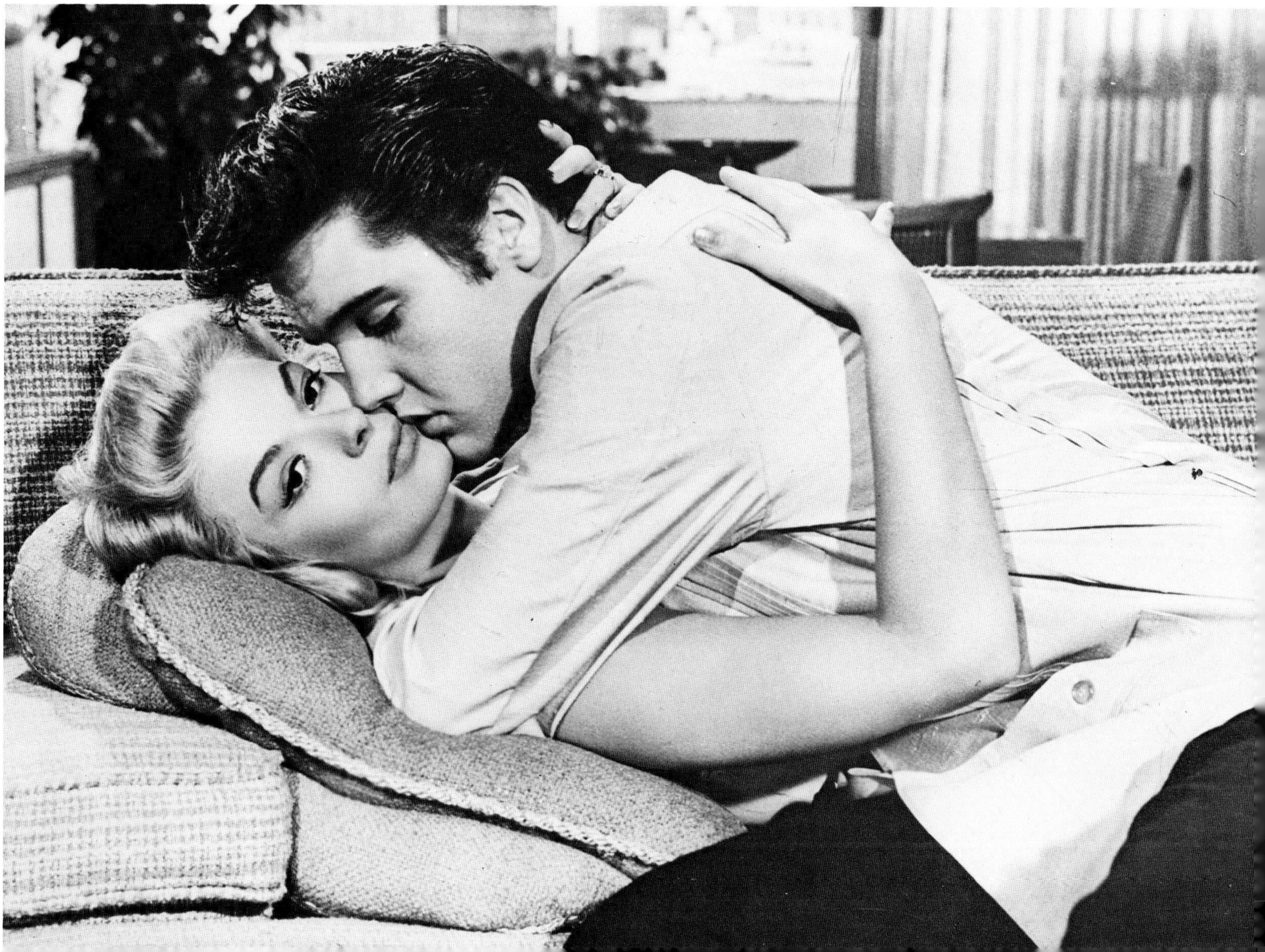

Viva Las Vegas

"Stick 'em up!" says Ann-Margaret to Elvis, clowning on the set of *Viva Las Vegas* (1964). It was widely rumored that their on-screen romance easily carried over into real life.

This was actually the cover of a bootleg album of songs from the film.

Roustabout   With Barbara Stanwyck and friend at the traveling circus of *Roustabout,* 1964.

Fun In Acapulco

On location with Ursula Andress
for *Fun In Acapulco*, 1963.

Change Of Habit

Elvis Presley, playing a community physician,
asks Mary Tyler Moore to choose between marriage
and her work as a nun in *Change Of Habit*, (1969),
his final Hollywood film before the triumphant
return to live performing.

Live A Little, Love A Little

With Great Dane, in *Live A Little, Love A Little*, 1968.

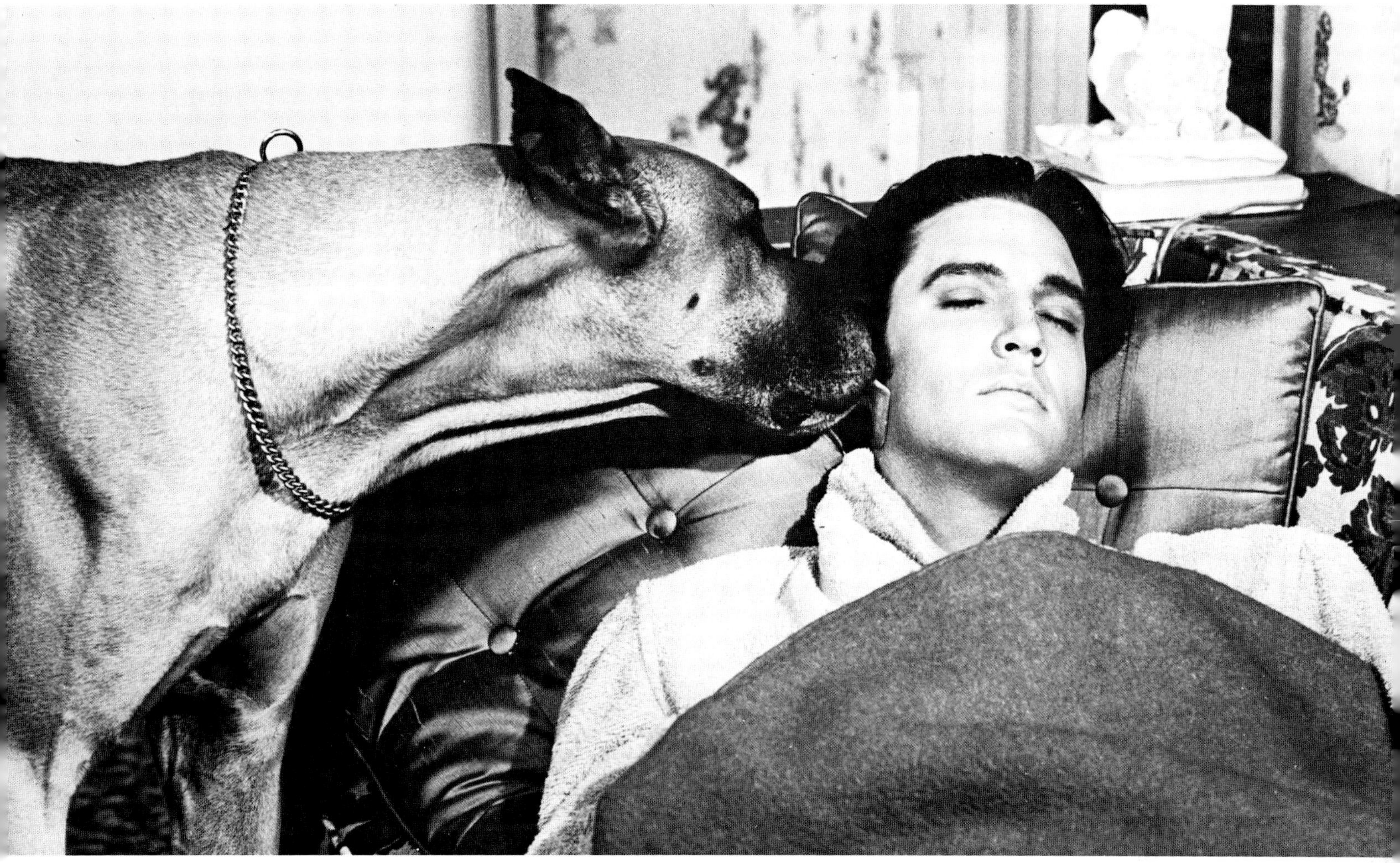

Charro

Charro, his twenty-ninth picture, filmed in July of 1968.

Love Me Tender
Classic portrait of Elvis during *Love Me Tender*, 1956.

In his first film, *Love Me Tender*, with co-star Debra Paget.

Kissin' Cousins

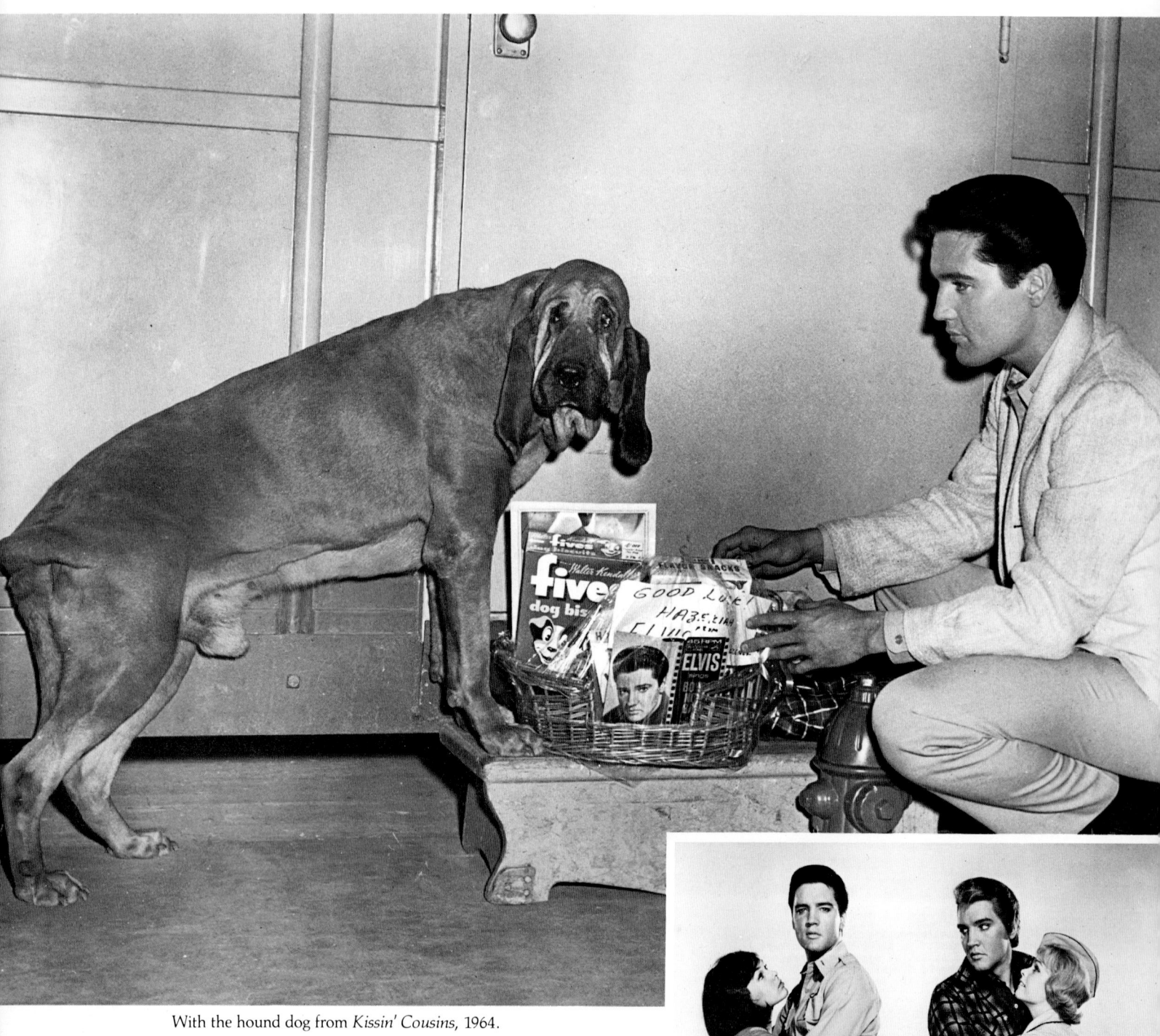

With the hound dog from *Kissin' Cousins*, 1964.

In double role for *Kissin' Cousins* with Yvonne Craig (right) and
Cynthia Pepper (left).

GRACELAND

Graceland, Elvis' Memphis mansion at 374 Elvis Presley Blvd.

Elvis poses at the newly installed "Music Gates" at Graceland, 1957.

Graceland kitchen: Ah, how much fried chicken and pork chops in onions and gravy, how many peanut butter and banana sandwiches were prepared here . . .

Fireplace, Graceland living room.

Living room with the peacocks in stained glass at Graceland.

The graves at Graceland.

Elvis photographed by Al Wertheimer outside of the Presley home, 1034 Audubon Drive, Memphis, before buying Graceland. The photo was taken at the period when Elvis was making his first records at RCA, as well as his first national television appearances — events which would alter his life drastically.

The "Lisa Marie," Elvis' $1.2 million Convair 880 touring jet.

The King's bathroom with the 24-karat gold sink.

May 4, 1982. Priscilla examines the awards and gold records in the Graceland den and announces the opening of the mansion to the public as a museum.

ELVIS & PRISCILLA

The Lord of Graceland, complete with cane, and his Lady.

Elvis and Priscilla on the night
Priscilla was introduced to Elvis at a
party in Bad Nauheim, Germany, 1959.

BOOK 248   405254

Marriage Certificate

State of Nevada | ss.   No. A 175632
County of Clark, |

This is to Certify that the undersigned   JUSTICE DAVID ZENOFF

did on the _____ 1st _____ day of _____ May _____ A.D. 196⁷ join in lawful

Wedlock   ELVIS ARON PRESLEY

of   MEMPHIS   State of   TENNESSEE

and   PRISCILLA ANN BEAULIEU

of   SHELBY   State of   TENNESSEE

with their mutual consent, in the presence of _Joe Esposito_

and _Marty Lacker_   who were witnesses.

Recorded at the Request of David Zenoff

Date   MAY 5 1967

In Book of Marriages, Clark County, Nevada,
Records, Paul E. Horn, Recorder.   JUSTICE, SUPREME COURT OF NEVADA

Fee $1.00 Indexed   GT   Deputy.   (Sign this in official capacity.)

MARRIAGE

Mr. and Mrs. Elvis Presley
in Hawaii, 1968.

Elvis and Priscilla cut the cake in the ballroom of the Aladdin Hotel,
May 1, 1967.

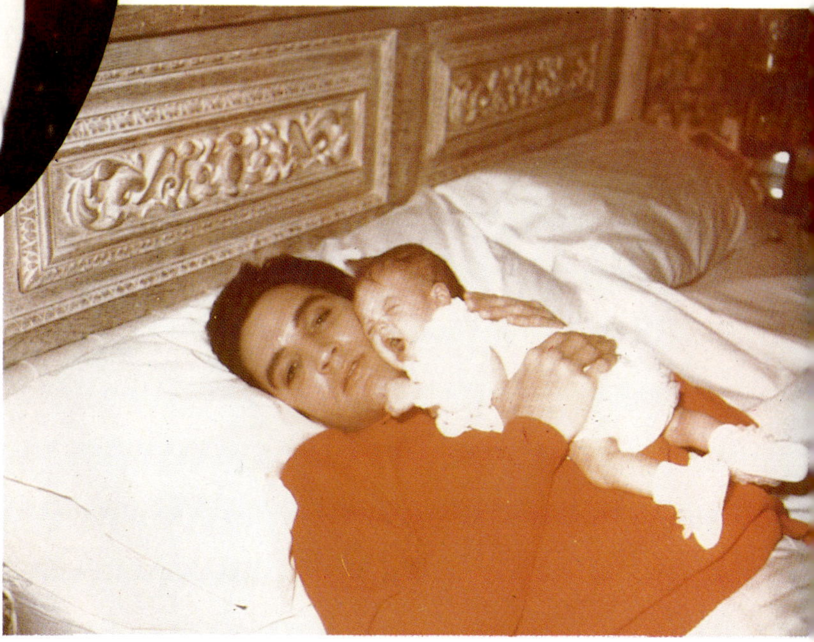

PRESLEY

Priscilla and Lisa Marie leave a NY restaurant in October, 1981. Two years later, Priscilla would join the cast of *Dallas* and begin her long-awaited book about her life with Elvis.

PERFORMING

Elvis, 1954, at the beginning.

From the documentary *Elvis: That's The Way It Is*, a record of his Vegas performances in 1970.

Performing "If I Can Dream" during the Christmas television special in 1968 that relaunched his career after years of forgettable films.

In black leather — the live segment of the 1968 Christmas television
special on NBC.

Performing at the *Louisiana Hayride* show, 1955, the Saturday night
country music broadcast from Shreveport, where Elvis appeared
regularly from 1954-55.

Elvis' first Las Vegas appearances, 1957. By all accounts, nobody knew what to make of him.

July 19, 1975, at Nassau Coliseum.

Doing the town in Vegas: left to right are "Ole Blue Eyes" himself, Elvis, bodyguard Sonny West, Priscilla Beaulieu Presley, and Nancy Sinatra (in lower right).

Elvis visits the Phillips. Dewey Phillips, at right, played Elvis' first record, "That's All Right (Mama)" on his Red, Hot and Blue radio show on WHBQ in Memphis.

With Anita Wood, 1958. Anita was a local Memphis TV and radio personality who dated Elvis the year before he went into the army. After his induction, many fans assumed she would be the girl he would marry upon his release. Alas, it wasn't meant to be . . . he would meet a little girl named Priscilla in Germany.

STARS

During *GI Blues*, Elvis hobnobs with (left to right) Hal Wallis, the Hollywood mogul who would produce nine of his films; and with Dean Martin and Shirley MacLaine, then filming *Some Came Running*. The occasion was Deano's birthday.

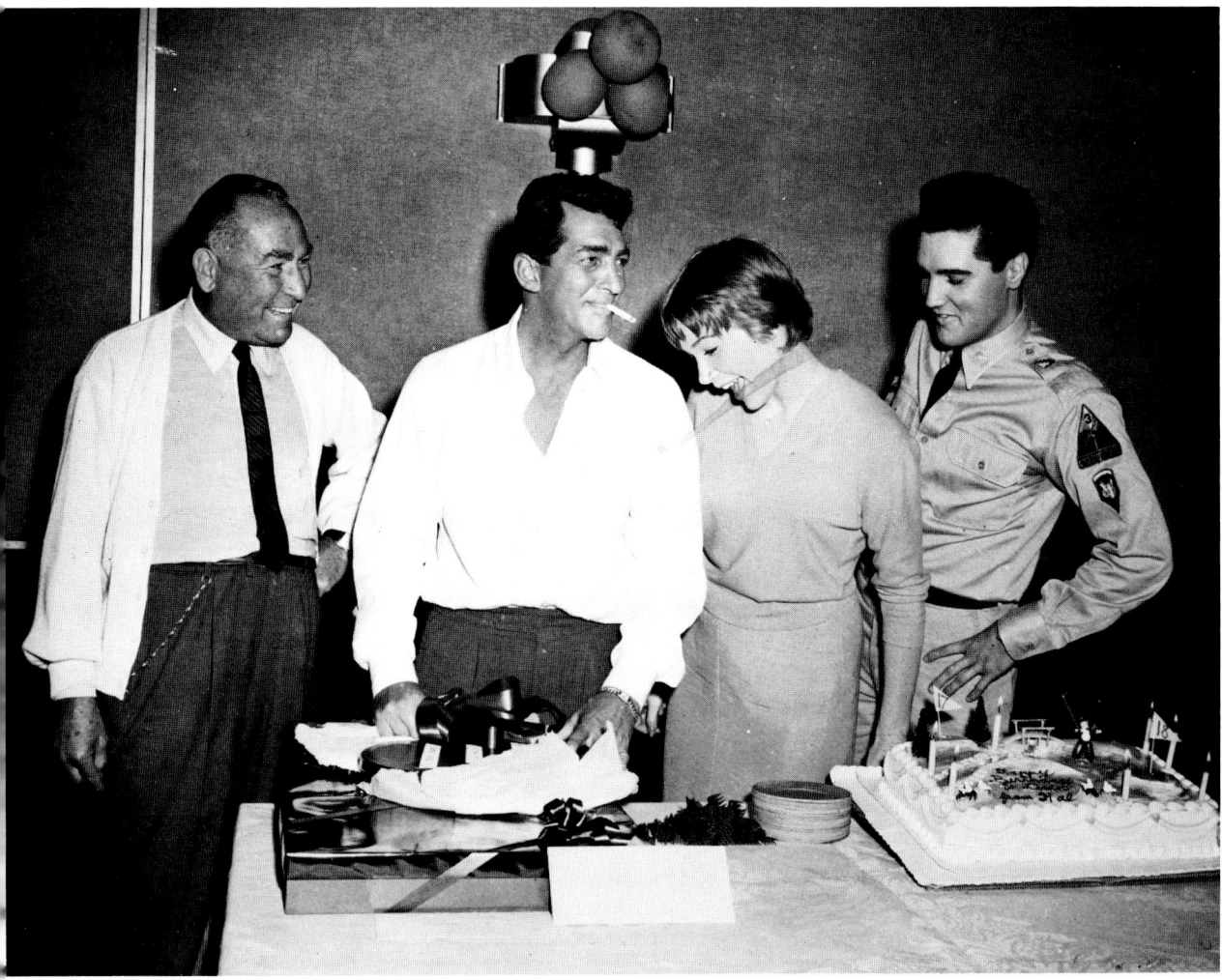

Elvis with teen singing sensation Brenda Lee.

In Hollywood, Elvis and his boys got to meet their true idols; in this case, football immortal Jim Brown, the ex-Cleveland Brown fullback turned actor. Memphis Mafia members include Elvis' cousin Billy Smith (far left), valet Richard David (behind Brown), and to Elvis' right, Joe Esposito and Marty Lacker.

True son of the South: Greeting Governor George Wallace of Alabama.

The Boss, resplendent in black cape, with shades and Dutch cigar, gives Glen Campbell an audience backstage in Las Vegas. Note the flashlight.

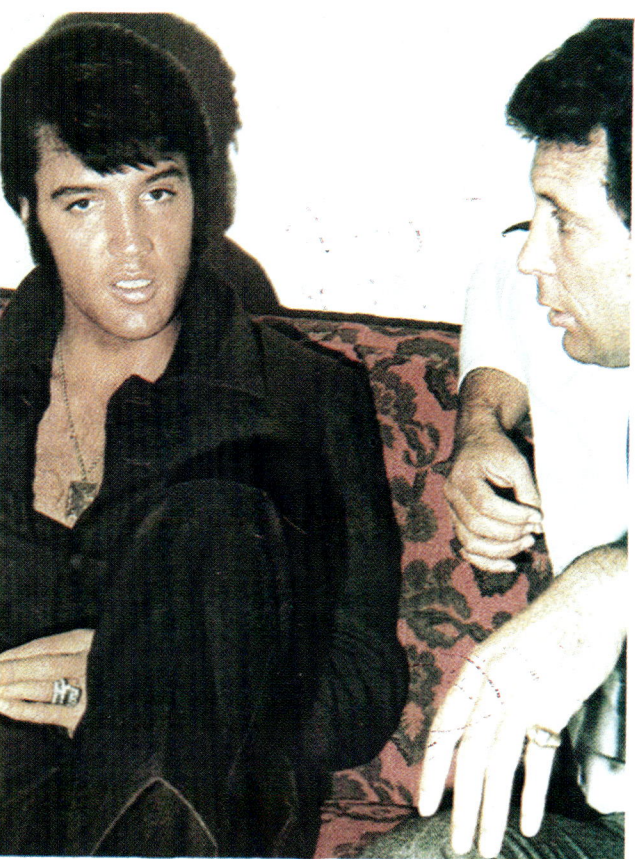

Friendly rivals in Las Vegas: Elvis and Tom Jones, circa 1972.

Elvis with then-Governor Jimmy Carter and Roslyn Carter, backstage at the Omni, Atlanta, 1973.

The King hanging out with the Greatest in Las Vegas. The two had a mutual fascination with each other. Whenever they met, Muhammed Ali would playfully cuff Elvis and shout, "Gawd, we got to be two of the best looking sumbitches in the world!" Elvis never disagreed.

Backstage at the Fountainbleu Hotel, Miami, March 26, 1960, for his Timex Special with Frank Sinatra, during which Frank essayed a few bars of "Love Me Tender" and Elvis did "Witchcraft."

Elvis in Hawaii for the filming of *Blue Hawaii*, spring of 1961. He fell in love with the place and would return many times over the years for vacations.

Backstage, Las Vegas. Elvis visits with his girlfriend Linda Thompson and her parents.

Filming *Follow That Dream*, in Florida, July of 1961.

Elvis in his motorcycle leathers for *Roustabout*, summer of 1964.

Elvis in shades and black mohair suit, followed by Vernon Presley. For a time, just as a kick, Elvis had his entire entourage dressing like this. Small wonder they were dubbed the "Memphis Mafia."

Elvis arrives in Hawaii to tape *Aloha from Elvis in Hawaii* in January of 1973, beamed via satellite to **a billion and a half people** throughout the world.

June 23, 1974, leaving the Philadelphia Hilton and thanking a fan who gave him a jar of Skippy peanut butter (certainly one of E's fave foodstuffs!). Surrounded by (left to right) Jerry Schilling, Joe Esposito, Red West, and Dick Grob. Vernon Presley brings up the rear.

Elvis being interviewed by WELO's Jack Crystal at the Mississippi-
Alabama State Fair at Tupelo, Miss., September, 1956. Elvis was
nineteen, returning triumphantly to his hometown.

Paparazzi Ron Galella's first photo of Elvis, spring of 1969, outside
ABC studios in Los Angeles.

Elvis as Glen Tyler in *Wild in the Country*, November of 1960.

Elvis as the womanizing photographer in *Live a Little, Love a Little*,
movie number twenty-eight, March of 1968.

In RCA Studios, rehearsing a number for *Jailhouse Rock*, 1957.

Press conference at the New York Hilton before a series of sold-out
Madison Square Garden performances, June 9, 1972. The historic
concerts would be recorded and released on a live concert LP.

CREDITS

Coordination: 2M Communications, Ltd.

Photo Research: Amanda Rubin

PHOTO CREDITS

Peter Bankers Collection: Inside Front Cover, 15 (bottom)

Dagmar/Shooting Star: 26 (bottom)

Ron Galella: Inside Back Cover, 16, 32, 40 (lower right), 45, 55, 56,59, 63

Harley Hatcher: Front Cover

Gay McRae Collection: 1, 2 (top & lower left), 3 (top), 4 (both), 5 (both), 6, 7 (top left & right), 8 (all), 9 (top), 10, 11 (all), 12, 14, 15 (top), 25, 26 (top), 27, 28, 29, 31 (both), 35 (both), 38-39, 40 (top left; lower left), 44 (all), 46 (all), 47 (both bottom), 48, 49 (top right; lower left), 51 (both), 54 (left & lower right), 57, 58

Neal Peters Collection: 3 (bottom), 9 (bottom), 13, 17 (both), 18 (both bottom), 19, 20 (both), 21 (both), 22, 23, 24 (both), 34 (bottom), 41, 42 (both) 43, 47 (top), 50, 53 (both), 60, 61, 62

Ebet Roberts: 30

The Silver Screen: Outside Back Cover

Star File: 54 (top right)

Jimmy Velvet, Elvis Presley Museum: 2 (lower right), 7 (lower left), 33, 34 (top), 36 (all), 37 (all), 40 (top right), 49 (top left & lower right), 52

Special thanks to Martin Torgoff, and to Gay McRae, the most loving fan in the world.